AMAZING MACHINES
EXCAVATORS

BY QUINN M. ARNOLD

CREATIVE EDUCATION • CREATIVE PAPERBACKS

Published by Creative Education and Creative Paperbacks
P.O. Box 227, Mankato, Minnesota 56002
Creative Education and Creative Paperbacks are imprints of
The Creative Company
www.thecreativecompany.us

Design by The Design Lab
Production by Chelsey Luther
Art direction by Rita Marshall
Printed in the United States of America

Photographs by Dreamstime (Artzzz, Matthew Heinrichs, Alexander
Ryabchun [Parrus]), Getty Images (Richard du Toit, Ethan Miller),
iStockphoto (Eduardo Luzzatti Buyé, CHUYN, nikitos77, PetarAn,
pic4you, stevecoleimages), Shutterstock (Dmitry Kalinovsky)

Library of Congress Cataloging-in-Publication Data
Names: Arnold, Quinn M., author.
Title: Excavators / Quinn M. Arnold.
Series: Amazing machines.
Includes bibliographical references and index.
Summary: A basic exploration of the parts, variations, and worksites
of excavators, the big digging machines. Also included is a pictorial
diagram of variations of excavators.
Identifiers: ISBN 978-1-60818-889-5 (hardcover) / ISBN 978-1-
62832-505-8 (pbk) / ISBN 978-1-56660-941-8 (eBook)
This title has been submitted for CIP processing under LCCN
2017937613.

CCSS: RI.1.1, 2, 4, 5, 6, 7; RI.2.2, 5, 6, 7, 10; RI.3.1, 5, 7, 8;
RF.1.1, 3, 4; RF.2.3, 4

First Edition HC 9 8 7 6 5 4 3 2 1
First Edition PBK 9 8 7 6 5 4 3 2 1

Table of Contents

Excavators are heavy machines. They are best known for their digging buckets. Early excavators scooped out waterways. They also worked in mines and rock **quarries**. Today, many excavators still dig up dirt, rocks, and **minerals**.

minerals substances that occur naturally in the ground

quarries large pits from which rocks, stone, or other building materials are dug out

An excavator bucket is at the end of an arm. The heavy machine turns to the left and right. It can reach a large area all around it.

Medium-sized excavators can reach about 30 feet (9.1 m).

Strong steel buckets come in different sizes. Many have teeth along the digging edge. Buckets scoop up heavy rocks or soil to fill dump trucks. Wider buckets may have a smooth edge. They clear and level land.

A bucket's teeth wear down over time and must be replaced.

Mini excavators work in tight spaces. Many can fit through a doorway. Mining excavators are massive. Their buckets scoop up several tons of materials. They load heavy mining dump trucks.

Mining excavator buckets can scoop 500 times more material than mini excavators'.

The orange peel grab attachment is commonly used in scrapyards.

An excavator's bucket can be taken off. Then other tools are attached. Heavy hammers break up pavement. Magnets lift scrap metal. Cutting tools chop down trees. **Grapples** hold pipes, logs, and other objects.

grapples hinged tools that open and close to grip objects

Most treads are made of strong steel, but some are made of thick rubber.

Most excavators move around on **caterpillar treads**. The wide treads grip the earth. They help the excavator work on hillsides. They keep it from sinking into soft dirt.

caterpillar treads bands looped around roller wheels to help heavy vehicles move

Excavators pull up

stumps and clear land. They dig holes for basements and foundations. They make trenches. Some excavators clear mud and weeds from rivers.

foundations the underground parts of buildings that support the structures

trenches long, narrow ditches

Some demolition excavators can reach more than 100 feet (30.5 m) high.

Many worksites need excavators.

The machines get the area ready for the new building or road. Some excavators **demolish** things. Their arm reaches up high to tear down buildings.

demolish to pull or knock down

Excavators work in many different places. Next time you are outside, look for an excavator. See what kind of work the heavy machine is doing!

A turntable allows an excavator to rotate without changing spots.

Excavator Blueprint

engine

cab

caterpillar tread

turntable

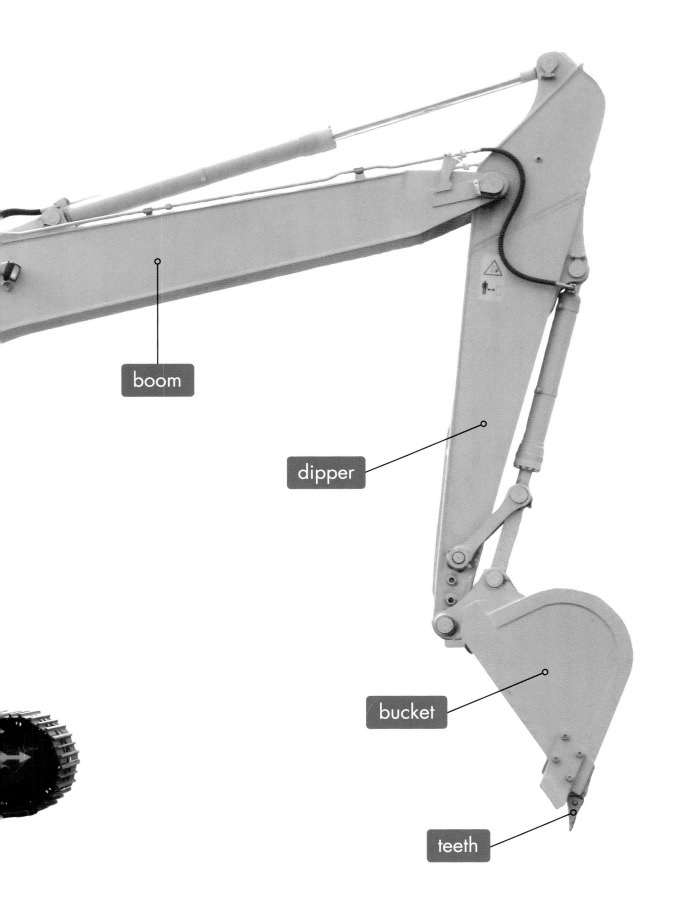

boom

dipper

bucket

teeth

Read More

Gordon, Nick. *Monster Diggers*. Minneapolis: Bellwether Media, 2014.

Schuh, Mari. *Diggers*. North Mankato, Minn.: Amicus, 2018.

Zeiger, Jennifer. *What Does It Do? Digger*. Ann Arbor, Mich.: Cherry Lake, 2011.

Websites

JCB: Excavators
http://www.jcbexplore.com/content/info_zone/jcb_machines/
Read more about excavators and mini excavators.

Kikki's Workshop
http://www.kenkenkikki.jp/e_index.html
Explore this site to learn more about construction machines and equipment.

Note: Every effort has been made to ensure that the websites listed above are suitable for children, that they have educational value, and that they contain no inappropriate material. However, because of the nature of the Internet, it is impossible to guarantee that these sites will remain active indefinitely or that their contents will not be altered.

Index